Common Core Les
The Civi
Key Battles & Events

By Carole Marsh

Published by Gallopade International, Inc.

Printed in the U.S.A. (Peachtree City, Georgia)

TABLE OF CONTENTS

G: Includes Graphic Organizer

GO: Graphic Organizer is also available 8½" x 11" online download at www.gallopade.com/client/go

(numbers above correspond to the graphic organizer numbers online)

The 1860 Election

Read the text and answer the questions.

Sectionalism between North and South increased as the country divided over the key issues of slavery and states' rights. Abraham Lincoln, a Republican from Kentucky, gained national attention for his stance against the spread of slavery to free-soil western territories.

The election of 1860 brought national discontent to a tipping point. After serving one term in the U.S. Senate, Lincoln secured the Republican nomination for President in the 1860 election. Lincoln ran on an anti-slavery platform that many people feared would cause Southern states to secede and move the country toward war. Democrats were divided between supporting Democratic candidate Stephen Douglas and Southern Democratic candidate John C. Breckinridge. With the Democratic Party divided, Lincoln won the election with nearly no support from the South.

By Lincoln's inauguration on March 4, 1861, seven states had seceded from the Union and formed the Confederate States of America. South Carolina was the first to secede, with others quickly following. In reaction, the Union quickly admitted the territories of Kansas, West Virginia, and Nevada to the Union as free-soil states. Four pro-slavery states did not declare secession, and remained "border states" between the Union and the Confederacy.

A month after Lincoln's inauguration, Confederate forces fired on the Union-held Fort Sumter in South Carolina.

1. What caused division between the North and the South?
2. Explain how the election of 1860 was a "tipping point" for war. Cite evidence from the text to support your answer.
3. What is the relationship between the 1860 election and the Civil War?
4. Use the text to number the following events in chronological order:
   _____ Confederate forces fire on Union forces at Fort Sumter
   _____ Abraham Lincoln secures the Republican Party's presidential nomination
   _____ South Carolina secedes from the Union
   _____ Abraham Lincoln defeats Breckinridge and Douglas in 1860 election
   _____ Three territories are admitted into the Union as free-soil states

Civil War Vocabulary

Use your own knowledge and other resources to complete the graphic organizer for each vocabulary word.

abolitionist
army
arsenal
battle
Confederacy
emancipation
fort
general
secession
strategy
surrender
troops
Union

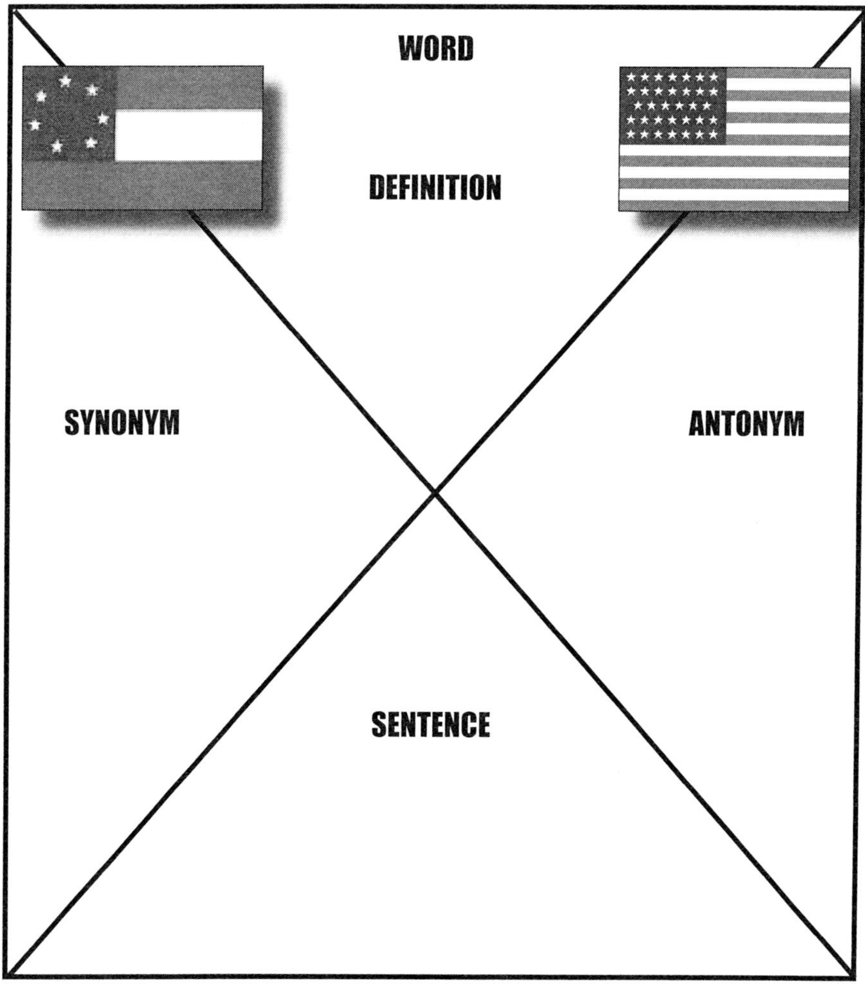

PRIMARY SOURCE ANALYSIS

Secession

This cartoon, titled "The Secession Movement" depicts the first states seceding from the Union to form the Confederacy.

Look at the cartoon and answer the questions

South Carolina	We go the whole hog—Old Hickory is dead, and now we'll have it.
Florida	Go it Carolina! We are the boys to "wreck" the Union.
Alabama	We go it blind, Cotton is King!
Mississippi	Down with the Union. Mississippi "repudiates her bonds."
Louisiana	Go it boys! We'll soon taste the "sweets" of secession.
Georgia	We have some doubts about "the end" of that road and think it expedient to deviate a little.

Courtesy of Library of Congress

1. Who is leading the charge? What is the significance of the order of the figures?
2. A. From what point of view is the cartoon drawn? Explain.
   B. What can you infer about the artist's opinion of secessionist states? What details from the cartoon support your conclusion?
3. What is the main message conveyed by this cartoon?
4. What can you infer about Alabama's reasons for seceding?
5. Why is Georgia separated from the other states? Explain.

COMPARISON OF SOURCES

General Robert E. Lee

Read the texts and answer the questions.

The Civil War is often called "the war between the states" and "a brother's war." When the South seceded from the Union, it divided families, tested loyalty, and forced many people to make difficult personal decisions. Brothers from the same family often fought on different sides of the war, and many Southerners previously in the U.S. Army resigned to fight with the new Confederacy.

Before the war, Robert E. Lee was a U.S. colonel. These letter excerpts explain his resignation from the U.S. Army.

Robert E. Lee to his sister, Ann Marshall (April 20, 1861):

With all my devotion to the Union, and the feeling of loyalty and duty of an American citizen, I have not been able to make up my mind to raise my hand against my relative, my children, my home. I have, therefore, resigned my commission in the [United States] Army…"

Robert E. Lee to U.S. General Winfield Scott:

[My resignation] would have been presented at once, but for the struggle it has cost me to separate myself from a service to which I have devoted all the best years of my life & all the ability I possessed.

Use the text to identify who or what is being described:

A. "a brother's war"
B. "my home"
C. "struggle"
D. "a service to which I have devoted all the best years of my life"

1. Explain how the Civil War "tested loyalty."

2. A. Why did Robert E. Lee resign from the U.S. Army?
   B. Why was he reluctant to resign?
   C. What can you infer about the timing of his resignation? Explain.
   D. Do you agree or disagree with his decision to resign? Why or why not?

READING INFORMATIONAL TEXT

First Shots of the Civil War

Read the texts and answer the questions.

Union Major Robert Anderson wrote, "Fort Sumter is a tempting prize, the value of which is well known to the Charlestonians, and once in their possession, with its ammunition and armament and walls uninjured and garrisoned properly, it would set our Navy at defiance, compel me to abandon this work, and give them the perfect command of this harbor."

Union Major Anderson took possession of Fort Sumter in December 1860, following South Carolina's secession from the Union. However, his position left him trapped by the Confederate military and with a limited supply of ammunition and vital supplies.

Francis Pickens, governor of South Carolina, instructed Anderson to leave the fort, but Anderson refused. South Carolina's growing military presence in the harbor prompted President Buchanan to send troops and supplies to aid Anderson. However, Confederate ships fired upon the Union supply ship and it retreated.

More states seceded from the Union and joined the Confederacy. On April 10, 1861, after learning that newly elected President Lincoln planned to send reinforcements to Fort Sumter, the Confederacy gave General Beauregard an order to attack "in such a manner as you may determine to reduce it," unless Anderson removed his troops from the fort.

Anderson refused to retreat. On April 12, the Confederate army attacked Fort Sumter. The Civil War had begun!

1. What can you infer about the location of Fort Sumter? Cite details from the text to support your answer.
2. A. What is meant by the phrase, tempting prize?
   B. Who was Fort Sumter a tempting prize for?
3. Why did Union Major Anderson take possession of Fort Sumter? Cite primary source evidence to support your answer.
4. What did the Confederacy mean when it ordered General Beauregard to attack "in such a manner as you determine to reduce it"?

PRIMARY SOURCE ANALYSIS

Telegram from Fort Sumter

Read the telegram and answer the questions.

S.S. BALTIC OFF SANDY HOOK APR. EIGHTEENTH. TEN THIRTY A.M. VIA NEW YORK.

HON.S.CAMERON. SECY.WAR. WASHN.

HAVING DEFENDED FORT SUMTER FOR THIRTY FOUR HOURS UNTIL THE QUARTERS WERE ENTIRELY BURNED THE MAIN GATES DESTROYED BY FIRE. THE GORGE WALLS SERIOUSLY INJURED. THE MAGAZINE SURROUNDED BY FLAMES AND ITS DOOR CLOSED FROM THE EFFECTS OF HEAT. FOUR BARRELLS AND THREE CARTRIDGES OF POWDER ONLY BEING AVAILABLE AND NO PROVISIONS REMAINING BUT PORK. I ACCEPTED TERMS OF EVACUATION OFFERED BY GENERAL BEAUREGARD BEING ON SAME OFFERED BY HIM ON THE ELEVENTH INST. PRIOR TO THE COMMENCEMENT OF HOSTILITIES AND MARCHED OUT OF THE FORT SUNDAY AFTERNOON THE FOURTEENTH INST. WITH COLORS FLYING AND DRUMS BEATING. BRINGING AWAY COMPANY AND PRIVATE PROPERTY AND SALUTING MY FLAG WITH FIFTY GUNS.

ROBERT ANDERSON. MAJOR FIRST ARTILLERY. COMMANDING.

1. Who was the author of the telegram? Who was the recipient?
2. A. What is the tone of the telegram?
   B. What words or phrases create the tone?
3. What can you infer about the author based on his description of the battle? Cite evidence from the text to support your answer.
4. What can you infer about the author based on his description of the retreat? Cite evidence from the text to support your answer.
5. A. What is the author's primary purpose for sending this telegram?
   B. Infer at least two underlying purposes for sending this telegram.
6. In your opinion, did the Robert Anderson have good reason to surrender Fort Sumter?

Leaders of the Civil War

Use what you know and other resources to complete the information for each influential leader in the Civil War. Then do the research and writing activity.

Leaders:	Who am I?	What did I do?	Union or Confederacy
Abraham Lincoln			
Thomas "Stonewall" Jackson			
Robert E. Lee			
Jefferson Davis			
Ulysses S. Grant			
William T. Sherman			
George McClellan			

Research & Writing

A. Individually or in small groups, use an online resource to do further research on one of the Civil War leaders from the organizer.
B. Create a digital presentation with pictures and information about the person's life before the war, during the war, and after the war. Describe his role in the Civil War and his influence on the war's outcome.
C. Share your presentation with your class.

Civil War Quotations

Summarize each quotation to complete the chart. Use the completed chart to answer the questions.

Civil War quotations:	What each quotation means to me:
"I have never advocated war except as a means of peace." — *General Ulysses S. Grant*	
"In giving freedom to the slave, we assure freedom to the free... We shall nobly save, or meanly lose, the last, best hope of earth." — *President Lincoln*	
"John Brown's <u>zeal</u> in the cause of freedom was infinitely superior to mine. Mine was as the taper light; his was as the burning sun. I could live for the slave; John Brown could die for him." — *Frederick Douglass*	

1. What is the main connection between these three quotations?
2. In what way do the quotes by Grant and Douglass express a similar point of view?
3. A. What does Douglass mean by <u>zeal</u>?
   B. What can you infer about Douglass' opinion of John Brown? Cite evidence from the text to support your answer.
4. For each person quoted, use the text to write a single word or phase that summarizes his point of view on war.

BONUS: When Douglass says, "I could live for the slave; John Brown could die for him," is his meaning literal or figurative? Explain.

COMPARISON OF PRIMARY SOURCES

Fighting for a Cause

Read the advertisement, read the quotation, and answer the questions.

This advertisement was placed by the U.S. War Department during the Civil War.

TO COLORED MEN!

FREEDOM,

Protection, Pay, and a Call to Military Duty!

On the 1st day of January, 1863, the President of the United States proclaimed FREEDOM to over THREE MILLIONS OF SLAVES. This decree is to be enforced by all the power of the Nation. On the 21st of July last he issued the following order:

PROTECTION OF COLORED TROOPS.

"WAR DEPARTMENT, ADJUTANT GENERAL'S OFFICE,
WASHINGTON, July 21.

"*General Order*, No. 233.

"The following order of the President is published for the information and government of all concerned:—

EXECUTIVE MANSION, WASHINGTON, July 30.

"'It is the duty of every Government to give protection to its citizens, of whatever class, color, or condition, and especially to those who are duly organized as soldiers in the public service. The law of nations, and the usages and customs of war, as carried on by civilized powers, permit no distinction as to color in the treatment of prisoners of war as public enemies. To sell or enslave any captured person on account of his color, is a relapse into barbarism, and a crime against the civilization of the age.

"'The Government of the United States will give the same protection to all its soldiers, and if the enemy shall sell or enslave any one because of his color, the offense shall be punished by retaliation upon the enemy's prisoners in our possession. It is, therefore, ordered, for every soldier of the United States, killed in violation of the laws of war, a rebel soldier shall be executed; and for every one enslaved by the enemy, or sold into slavery, a rebel soldier shall be placed at hard labor on the public works, and continued at such labor until the other shall be released and receive the treatment due to prisoners of war.

"'ABRAHAM LINCOLN.'"

"By order of the Secretary of War.

"E. D. TOWNSEND, Assistant Adjutant General."

That the President is in earnest the rebels soon began to find out, as witness the following order from his Secretary of War:

Courtesy of the National Archives

This quotation was written by Frederick Douglass, a leader of the abolitionist movement.

> "Once let the black man get upon his person the brass letter, U.S., let him get an eagle on his button, and a musket on his shoulder and bullets in his pocket, there is no power on earth that can deny that he has earned the right to citizenship."
>
> — Frederick Douglass

PART A: Use the advertisement to answer these questions.

1. Who is the primary audience addressed by this advertisement?
2. Where would the advertisement most likely have been placed?
3. What is the purpose of this advertisement?
4. How does it attempt to achieve its purpose?
5. In your opinion, is this advertisement effective? Why or why not? Predict how a freed slave might react to this advertisement.

PART B: Use the quotation to answer these questions.

6. What do the "brass letter" and the "eagle on his button" symbolize?
7. Summarize the main message of this quotation in your own words.
8. What can you infer about Frederick Douglass' opinion of freed slaves serving in the Union army?

PART C: Use both primary sources to answer these questions.

9. Identify the common theme shared by both primary sources.
10. Use the Venn diagram to compare and contrast the two primary sources.

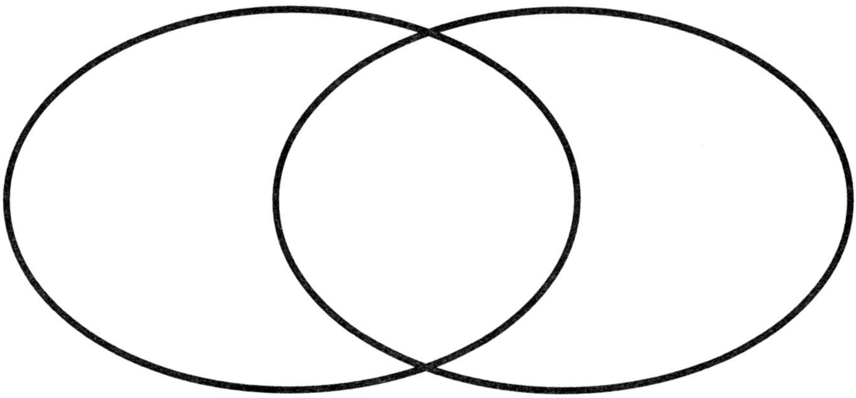

Writing Prompt

Black soldiers faced a much greater danger than whites when captured by Confederate troops. If captured by the Confederacy, officers of black regiments faced severe punishment and black soldiers faced brutal physical abuse, even execution.

Write an argument to convince freed slaves to serve in the U.S. (Union) Army, or to convince them not to. What do they stand to win? What do they stand to lose? Use details and cite evidence from the primary sources to support your argument.

Civil War

Complete the graphic organizer with key causes, events, and effects of the Civil War.

Causes:

Events:

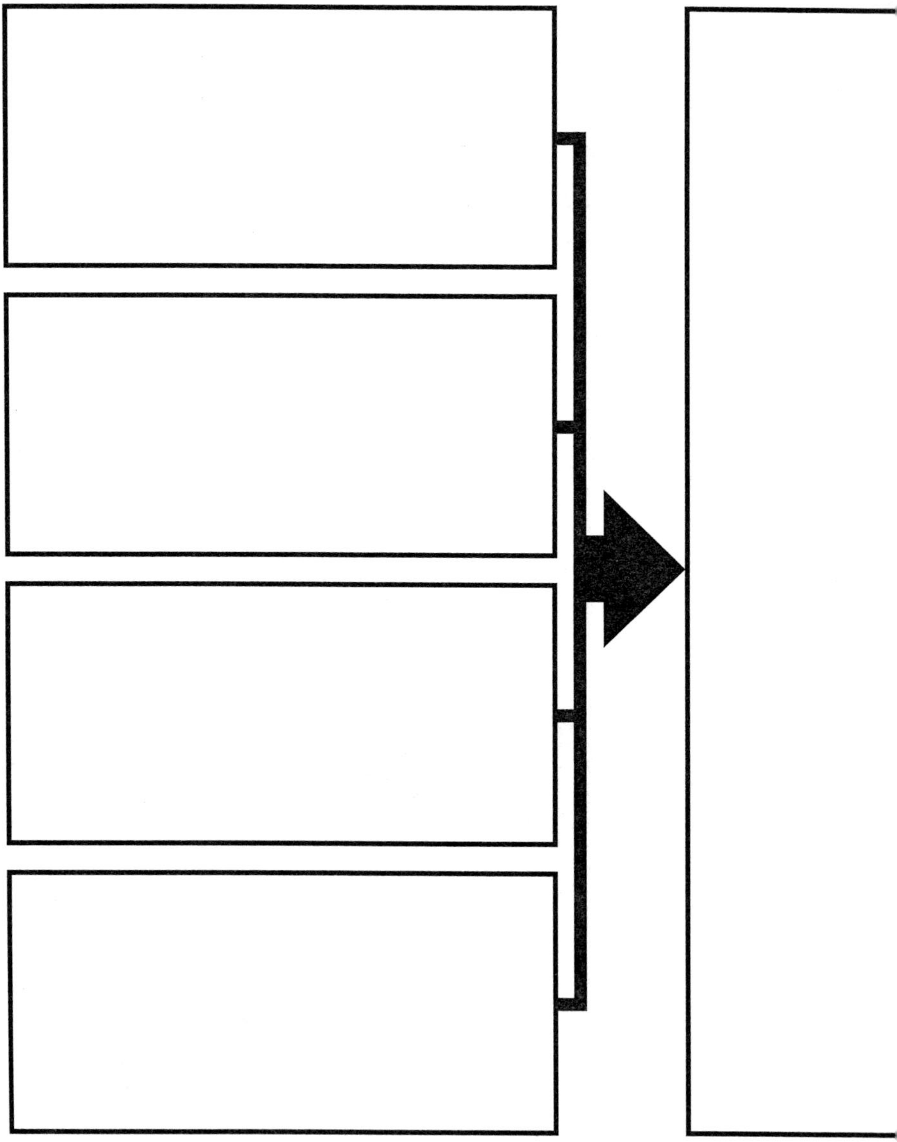

Effects:

Battle Strategies

The Union had several natural advantages over the Confederacy. At the start of the Civil War, the Union already had a well-trained military and a competent navy. The North also had a higher population, and the North's industrialized economy gave the Union access to materials and war supplies. The South's economy, by comparison, was primarily agricultural. The South's economy relied on exporting cotton and other cash crops to Europe while lacking the materials and supplies usually provided by the North. In addition, the Confederacy had no navy and was forced to quickly recruit, train, and supply the soldiers for the Confederate army.

Union General Winfield Scott advised Lincoln to use the South's disadvantages against them. Scott suggested the Union isolate the Confederacy by blockading all Southern seaports to cripple the South's economy. Scott also suggested controlling the Mississippi River to further constrict the Confederacy. General Scott's plan was heavily criticized because it did not involve an aggressive attack strategy. It was called the "anaconda plan" because it planned to "squeeze" the South into surrendering.

Instead, Lincoln ordered a direct attack on the Confederacy. However, in 1864, Union General Ulysses S. Grant used General Scott's strategy to help win the Civil War. General Grant won control of the Mississippi River and used blockades to cut off all shipments to the Confederacy. By then, the Confederacy was lacking most supplies needed to continue fighting.

The primary goal of the Confederate strategy was to defend the new nation from the Union attack. Confederate President Jefferson Davis was aware of the Confederacy's disadvantages. He thought it best to protect the Confederate states by concentrating his forces against tactical advancements of the invading Union army.

Many Southerners, however, were not content waiting for the enemy to attack. They made the argument that "the best defense is a good offense." Thus, when opportunity presented itself, Jefferson Davis allowed his generals to attack on offensive campaigns, at several points even invading the North. Jefferson Davis called his battle strategy an "offensive-defensive" strategy. However, the South did not have enough soldiers or supplies to defend against the Union forever.

PART A: Use the text to answer these questions.

1. A. What type of economy existed in the North?
   B. How did the North's economy affect the Union?
2. A. What type of economy existed in the South?
   B. How did the South's economy affect the Confederacy?

PART B: Interpret the cartoon and the text to answer these questions.

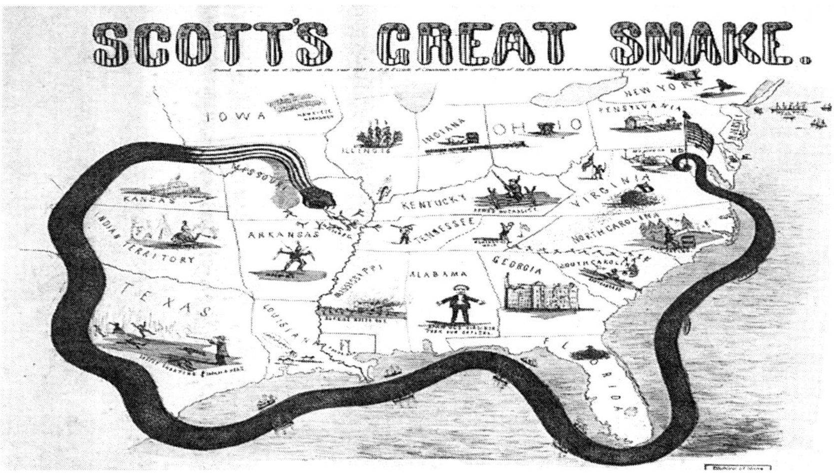

3. What types of information are shown in this cartoon?
4. What does "Scott's Great Snake" represent in this cartoon?
5. A. What is represented by the part of the snake in the water?
   B. What is represented by the part of the snake on land?
6. What was the purpose of "Scott's Great Snake"?
7. How did General Winfield Scott plan to use the South's disadvantages against the Confederacy?
8. How did "Scott's Great Snake" impact the Civil War?

PART C: Use the text to answer these questions.

9. What was the purpose of Jefferson Davis' strategy?
10. Use the text to explain the phrase "offensive-defensive."
11. Do you agree or disagree that "the best defense is a good offense"? Use logical reasoning and evidence from the text to support your opinion.
12. In your opinion, which strategy was more effective—Union or Confederate? Cite evidence from the text to support your opinion.

Emancipation Proclamation

Read the text and answer the questions.

President Lincoln first proposed the idea for the Emancipation Proclamation to his advisors in the summer of 1862. He thought that if Confederate slaves were freed, the Confederacy could no longer use their labor. He also predicted that freed slaves would join the Union cause. However, Lincoln waited for an event that would prove the Union could support such a bold proclamation.

On September 17, 1862, at the Battle of Antietam, Union and Confederate forces clashed on Union soil in the bloodiest single-day battle in American history. The battle resulted in a Union victory, giving President Lincoln the confidence and opportunity to issue the Emancipation Proclamation.

On January 1, 1863, the Emancipation Proclamation declared that all slaves in the ten rebelling Confederate states were free. This applied to 3.1 million slaves in the Confederate states but did not apply to slaves in the Union-sided Border states. Additionally, freedom to all slaves depended on the Union winning the Civil War. With every Union victory in the South, more Confederate slaves were given their freedom.

In effect, the Emancipation Proclamation changed the character of the war. It expanded the focus of the Civil War to the emancipation of slaves as well as the preservation of the Union. The Proclamation also allowed black men to enter the Union army and navy. By the end of the Civil War, approximately 200,000 black men had joined the Union cause for freedom.

1. A. Use a dictionary to define emancipation and proclamation.
   B. Use these definitions to write your own definition of Emancipation Proclamation.
2. Why did President Lincoln wait until after the Battle of Antietam to issue the Emancipation Proclamation?
3. A. What did the Emancipation Proclamation mean for slaves?
   B. Identify at least two ways the power of the Proclamation was limited. Cite evidence from the text to support each answer.
4. How did the Emancipation Proclamation affect the the Civil War?

Identifying Major Events

Fill in the missing information to complete the chart about major events of the Civil War. Use your own knowledge and secondary sources to complete the activity. Some of the information is included.

Date/Location	Event	Outcome	Significance
			Marked the beginning of the Civil War
		Confederate victory; Beauregard retreats back to Washington, D.C.	
April 6-7, 1862 in Tennessee			
			Union gains command of the Mississippi River
	The Battle of Gettysburg		
September 2 through December 22, 1864 in Georgia			
			End of the war

PRIMARY SOURCE ANALYSIS

Battle of Gettysburg

Look at the painting, read the Gettysburg Address, and answer the questions.

Painting of the Battle of Gettysburg by Thure de Thulstrup, 1887

Courtesy of Library of Congress

---

1. Write a title for the painting to express the main idea.
2. In your own words, describe the battle formations used in the Civil War as shown in the painting.
3. What can you infer about the battle conditions experienced by soldiers at Gettysburg? Cite evidence from both sources.
4. How many years is "four-score and seven years" in section 1 of the text? To what event is Lincoln referring?
5. Describe the tone of the Gettysburg Address. Cite words and phrases that help identify the tone. What else contributes to the tone?

The Gettysburg Address *by President Abraham Lincoln; November 19, 1863.*

1) Four score and seven years ago our fathers brought forth, upon this continent, a new nation, conceived in liberty, and dedicated to the proposition that "all men are created equal."

2) Now we are engaged in a great civil war, testing whether that nation, or any nation so conceived, and so dedicated, can long endure.

3) We are met on a great battle field of that war. We have come to dedicate a portion of it, as a final resting place for those who died here, that the nation might live. This we may, in all propriety do. But, in a larger sense, we can not dedicate—we can not consecrate—we can not hallow, this ground—The brave men, living and dead, who struggled here, have hallowed it, far above our poor power to add or detract. The world will little note, nor long remember what we say here; while it can never forget what they did here.

4) It is rather for us, the living, we here be dedicated to the great task remaining before us —that, from these honored dead we take increased devotion to that cause for which they here, gave the last full measure of devotion—that we here highly resolve these dead shall not have died in vain; that the nation, shall have a new birth of freedom, and that government of the people by the people for the people, shall not perish from the earth.

Courtesy of the National Archives and Records Administration

---

6. A. Identify at least two phrases that Lincoln borrowed from the Declaration of Independence.
   B. What effect does Lincoln achieve by using phrases from the Declaration of Independence?
7. Analyze section 3 and the meaning of "This we may, in all propriety do."
   A. What is Lincoln saying can be done?
   B. What is Lincoln saying cannot be done? Why?
8. What is meant by "the great task remaining before us" in section 4?
9. What is meant by "we here highly resolve these dead shall not have died in vain" in section 4?

Sherman's Total War Strategy

Read the text and answer the questions.

Union General William Tecumseh Sherman's capture of Atlanta on September 2, 1864, was an important victory for the Union. Once Atlanta was won, Sherman and his army of 60,000 men continued to Savannah on a destructive "March to the Sea."

The biggest impact was that Atlanta, a railroad hub and industrial center, could no longer provide the Confederacy with food and weapons. As Sherman passed through Georgia, he used a "scorched earth" policy, otherwise known as "total war." His troops stole food and livestock, ripped up railroad tracks, and burned the crops and houses of civilians. Sherman's scorched earth tactics destroyed Confederate supplies and discouraged Georgians from supporting the Confederate war effort. Sherman explained that the Union was "not only fighting hostile armies, but a hostile people."

One of Sherman's men described the purpose of the destruction: "...we must war upon and destroy the organized rebel forces—must cut off their supplies, destroy their communications... and produce among the people of Georgia a thorough conviction of the personal misery which attends war, and the utter helplessness and inability of their 'rulers' to protect them...If that terror and grief and even want shall help to paralyze their husbands and fathers who are fighting us...it is mercy in the end."

1. Why was Sherman's conquest of Atlanta important to the Union?
2. A. Write a definition for "total war" in your own words.
   B. Use the text to explain why Sherman's march is called "total war."
3. Analyze each statement and identify whether it **most likely** expresses the point of view of a soldier in Sherman's army or a Georgia civilian.
   ___________"It is our duty to protect our homes from the invaders."
   ___________"I pity their families and homes, but this war must be won."
   ___________"A rebel state and a rebel people will receive no soft hand."
4. A. Who did Union soldiers cause to feel "personal misery" and "utter helplessness"? Describe two ways this benefited the Union.
5. Do you agree or disagree that Sherman's total war tactics were "mercy in the end"? Why or why not?

Sherman's Christmas Gift

During Sherman's March to the Sea, Sherman was out of touch with President Lincoln for nearly a month. On December 22, 1864, Sherman sent President Lincoln a telegram presenting the captured city of Savannah as a Christmas gift to Lincoln. This letter is President Lincoln's reply to General Sherman.

Read the letter and answer the questions.

Many, many thanks for your Christmas gift - the capture of Savannah. When you were leaving Atlanta for the Atlantic coast, I was anxious, if not fearful; but feeling that you were the better judge, and remembering that 'nothing risked, nothing gained' I did not interfere. Now, the undertaking being a success, the honor is all yours; for I believe none of us went farther than to acquiesce. And taking the work of Gen. Thomas into the count, as it should be taken, it is indeed a great success. Not only does it afford the obvious and immediate military advantage; but, in showing to the world that your army could be divided, putting the stronger part to an important new service, and yet leaving enough to vanquish the old opposing force of the whole—Hood's army—it brings those who sat in darkness, to see a great light. But what next? I suppose it will be safer if I leave Gen. Grant and yourself to decide. Please make my grateful acknowledgements to your whole army, officers and men.

1. Use the letter to infer whether each statement is **true** or **false**. Cite evidence from the letter to support your answer.

   ___________From the start, Lincoln was confident in Sherman's victory.

   ___________Sherman faced risks by dividing his army.

   ___________Lincoln was grateful for the gift of victory over Savannah.

   ___________Lincoln ordered Sherman's next movement.

2. Use the text to make five inferences about President Lincoln as commander-in-chief. Cite words or phrases from the letter to support each inference.

3. In your opinion, is the proverb "nothing risked, nothing gained" appropriate to describe Sherman's March to the Sea? Use evidence from the text to support your opinion.

Surrender at Appomattox

On April 3, 1865, after four long, bloody years, Union troops finally captured the Confederate capital of Richmond, Virginia. The Confederate government fled the city. The two generals arranged terms of surrender at a courthouse in Appomattox, Virginia.

Read the letters and answer the questions.

"The results of the last week must convince you of the hopelessness of further resistance on the part of the Army of Northern Virginia in this struggle. I feel that it is so, and regard it as my duty to shift from myself the responsibility of any further effusion of blood by asking of you the surrender of that portion of the Confederate States army known as the Army of Northern Virginia."

Ulysses S. Grant to Robert E. Lee
April 7, 1865

"I have received your note of this date. Though not entertaining the opinion you express of the hopelessness of further resistance on the part of the Army of Northern Virginia, I reciprocate your desire to avoid useless effusion of blood, and therefore, before considering your proposition, ask the terms you will offer on condition of its surrender."

—Robert E. Lee to Ulysses S. Grant
April 7, 1865

1. Describe the style of the two letters. Cite text from each letter to support your answer.
2. Use a dictionary and the letters to explain the meaning of "effusion of blood" as used in both letters.
3. A. What does Grant's letter try to convince Lee to do?
   B. What reasons does Grant use to support his request?
4. A. On what point do Grant and Lee agree?
   B. On what point do Grant and Lee disagree?
5. A. Summarize the main message of Lee's response in your own words.
   B. If you were Grant, what would you infer from Lee's response? Explain.

Civil War Casualties 1861-1865

Analyze the table and answer the questions.

Civil War Casualties	**Confederate**	**Union**
Killed in action or mortally wounded	94,000	110,100
Died of disease	164,000	224,580
Died as prisoners of war	31,000	30,192
Total Deaths	289,000	389,753
Wounded in Action	194,026	275,175
Total Casualties	483,026	664,928

1. What is the purpose of the table?
2. What is meant by the word "casualties" as it is used in the table?
3. Which side suffered more casualties—Union or Confederate?
4. A. What was the primary cause of death of soldiers in the Civil War?
   B. What can you infer from this data?
5. Based on what you know about the outcome of the Civil War, what can you infer from the data in the table?
6. Research medical practices during the Civil War. Write an informational essay describing the methods and shortcomings of Civil War medicine. How is this reflected in the data in the chart?

Correlations to Common Core State Standards

For your convenience, correlations are listed page-by-page, and for the entire book!

This book is correlated to the Common Core State Standards for English Language Arts grades 3-8, and to Common Core State Standards for Literacy in History, Science, & Technological Subjects grades 6-8.

Correlations are highlighted in gray.

PAGE #	READING *Includes:* RI: Reading Informational Text RH: Reading History/Social Studies	WRITING *Includes:* W: Writing WHST: Writing History/Social Studies, Science, & Technical Subjects	LANGUAGE *Includes:* L: Language LF: Language Foundational Skills	SPEAKING & LISTENING *Includes:* SL: Speaking & Listening
2	RI RH . **1 2 3 4 5** 6 7 **8** 9 **10**	W WHST . 1 **2** 3 **4** 5 6 7 8 **9 10**	L LF . 1 2 3 **4 5 6**	SL . 1 2 3 4 5 6
3	RI RH . 1 2 3 **4 5** 6 7 8 9 **10**	W WHST . 1 2 3 **4** 5 **6** 7 **8** 9 10	L LF . 1 2 3 **4 5 6**	SL . 1 2 3 4 5 6
4	RI RH . **1 2 3 4 5 6 7** 8 9 **10**	W WHST . 1 **2** 3 **4** 5 6 7 8 **9 10**	L LF . 1 2 3 **4 5 6**	SL . 1 2 3 4 5 6
5	RI RH . **1** 2 **3 4 5 6** 7 **8 9 10**	W WHST . **1 2** 3 **4** 5 6 7 **8 9 10**	L LF . 1 2 **3 4 5 6**	SL . 1 2 3 4 5 6
6	RI RH . **1 2 3 4 5 6** 7 **8 9 10**	W WHST . 1 **2** 3 **4** 5 6 7 8 **9 10**	L LF . 1 2 3 **4 5 6**	SL . 1 2 3 4 5 6
7	RI RH . **1 2 3** 4 **5 6** 7 **8** 9 **10**	W WHST . **1 2** 3 **4** 5 6 7 8 **9 10**	L LF . 1 2 **3 4 5 6**	SL . 1 2 3 4 5 6
8	RI RH . 1 **2** 3 4 **5** 6 **7** 8 9 10	W WHST . 1 **2** 3 **4 5 6 7 8** 9 **10**	L LF . 1 **2 3 4** 5 **6**	SL . **1 2** 3 **4 5 6**
9	RI RH . **1 2 3 4 5 6** 7 **8 9 10**	W WHST . **1 2** 3 **4** 5 6 7 **8 9 10**	L LF . 1 2 3 **4** 5 **6**	SL . 1 2 3 4 5 6
10-11	RI RH . **1 2 3 4 5 6 7 8 9 10**	W WHST . **1 2 3 4 5** 6 7 8 **9 10**	L LF . 1 2 **3 4** 5 6	SL . 1 2 3 4 5 6
12-13	RI RH . 1 **2** 3 4 **5** 6 **7** 8 9 10	W WHST . 1 **2** 3 **4** 5 6 **7** 8 9 **10**	L LF . 1 2 3 4 5 6	SL . 1 2 3 4 5 6
14-15	RI RH . **1 2 3 4 5 6 7 8 9 10**	W WHST . **1 2** 3 **4** 5 6 7 8 **9 10**	L LF . 1 2 3 **4 5 6**	SL . 1 2 3 4 5 6
16	RI RH . **1** 2 **3 4 5** 6 7 8 **9 10**	W WHST . 1 **2** 3 **4** 5 6 7 8 **9 10**	L LF . 1 2 3 **4** 5 **6**	SL . 1 2 3 4 5 6
17	RI RH . 1 2 3 4 **5** 6 **7** 8 9 **10**	W WHST . 1 **2** 3 **4 5 6 7 8** 9 **10**	L LF . 1 2 **3 4** 5 6	SL . 1 2 3 4 5 6
18-19	RI RH . **1 2 3 4 5 6 7 8 9 10**	W WHST . 1 **2** 3 **4** 5 6 7 8 **9 10**	L LF . 1 2 3 **4 5 6**	SL . 1 2 3 4 5 6
20	RI RH . **1** 2 **3 4 5 6** 7 **8** 9 **10**	W WHST . **1 2 3 4** 5 6 7 **8 9 10**	L LF . 1 2 **3 4 5 6**	SL . 1 2 3 4 5 6
21	RI RH . **1 2 3** 4 **5** 6 7 **8** 9 **10**	W WHST . 1 **2** 3 **4** 5 6 7 8 **9 10**	L LF . 1 2 3 **4 5** 6	SL . 1 2 3 4 5 6
22	RI RH . **1 2 3 4 5 6** 7 **8 9 10**	W WHST . 1 **2** 3 **4** 5 6 7 8 9 10	L LF . 1 2 3 **4 5 6**	SL . 1 2 3 4 5 6
23	RI RH . **1 2 3 4** 5 6 **7** 8 **9 10**	W WHST . 1 **2** 3 **4 5 6 7 8** 9 **10**	L LF . 1 2 3 **4** 5 **6**	SL . 1 2 3 4 5 6
COMPLETE BOOK	RI RH . **1 2 3 4 5 6 7 8 9 10**	W WHST . **1 2 3 4 5 6 7 8 9 10**	L LF . 1 **2 3 4 5 6**	SL . **1 2** 3 **4 5 6**

For the complete Common Core standard identifier, combine your grade + "." + letter code above + "." + number code above.

In addition to the correlations indicated here, the activities may be adapted or expanded to align to additional standards and to meet the diverse needs of your unique students!